THE FREELANCER'S GUIDE TO GETTING STARTED

THE PLANS YOU NEED TO LAUNCH A SUCCESSFUL FREELANCE CAREER

CURTIS MCHALE

HAZEL ST PRESS

978-1-7753364-7-1 ISBN (Hardcover Print Edition)

978-1-7753364-5-7 ISBN (Paperback Print Edition)

978-1-7753364-6-4 ISBN (Electronic Edition)

All photographs by Curtis McHale unless otherwise noted.

First printing August 2018

Published by Hazel Street Press

PO Box 2207 Stn Main

Chilliwack, BC

V2R 1A6

Canada

Visit: https://curtismchale.ca

GET THE AUDIOBOOK FOR FREE!

Just to say thanks for purchasing this book I want to give you a copy of the audiobook for FREE!

To download go to:

https://curtismchale.ca/recommends/fggs-audio

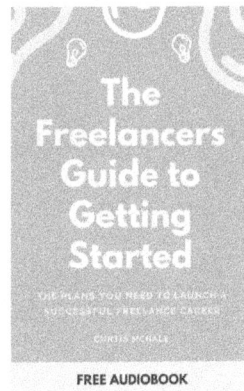

The
Freelancers
Guide to
Getting
Started

THE PLANS YOU NEED TO LAUNCH A
SUCCESSFUL FREELANCE CAREER

CURTIS MCHALE

FREE AUDIOBOOK

INTRODUCTION

So you think you want to be a freelancer? You're dreaming about those laptop on the beach pictures, or maybe the pictures of a fancy coffee and a laptop in some far flung place. Either way, the freedom is something you long for as you sit in your cubicle listening to coworkers talk about things you don't care about.

The problem that most freelancer's encounter is that they didn't realize they had to run a business. It wasn't all about fancy pictures posted to social media accounts. Many of those photos you idolized were done by people whose business is...to share fancy photos so that they can be "influencers".

That's where The Freelancer's Guide to Getting Started is going to help you. Over the 11 chapters of this book I'm going to walk you through the things you need to think about if you want to launch a successful business, and keep it running. We're going to cover everything from the fact that you run a sales and marketing business, no matter what service you sell to clients, to the fact that you need to learn how to handle your money.

As we go through each of these chapters I'm going to tell you exactly what has worked for me as I've kept my freelance business going for over 10 years. I'm going to share with you exactly what has worked for my coaching clients as they built sustainable freelance businesses.

Let's take Danny as an example. When he started he was just scraping by, which sucked because he is a great programmer. The thing is he didn't value himself properly (Chapter 5). He didn't budget his business well (Chapter 4). He didn't set good goals (Chapter 7). He was never realistic with the time he could work in the day, drastically overestimating it (Chapter 2).

Once we worked together through the material in this book, Danny started earning 6-figures a year. That's not just revenue, he was able to pay himself a 6-figure salary, and not work more than 40 hours a week.

You can do this too, if you have a plan. The Freelancer's Guide to Getting Started is going to help you have that plan. It's going to set your thinking straight about where you need to focus as you get your business going. It's going to give you budgeting strategies and ways to set boundaries with clients. You're going to understand how to price your services well, and get your clients to pay those prices because you provide such high value.

If you take the time to read this, you'll get paid on time and for the rates you deserve.

Don't be the freelancer that struggles through feast and famine lamenting the poor clients you get. Read this book and start to take your business seriously so you can succeed. Can you really wait to start building that 6-figure business you want?

ONE

WHAT YOU NEED TO BE READY TO FREELANCE

* * *

So you purchased the book and aren't yet freelancing. I'm sure that you didn't want to hear that you're not ready yet. The simple fact is that many people I know that start freelancing were not ready. They got caught up in the moment of a few good clients and decided that they didn't need this job thing. Most of them were back doing something they didn't love in a year, or less, and were starting to believe the fallacy that they weren't cut out for running a business.

If you're not sure how to run your business yet, and don't have a proper safety net then you're greatly increasing your chance of failure. I don't want you to fail. **You don't want you to fail**. Taking just a bit longer to get this set up will give you a huge leg up in making your business fly.

Freelancing was a life changing experience for me. One that is amazing. I want you to experience that awesome change with as few of the rocky parts as possible.

This chapter will walk you through the crucial things you need to make sure you've thought about before you dive into the freelance life. If you don't take the time to make sure these things are covered, you're increasing your chances of freelance failure.

Savings

Hopefully this doesn't come as news to you, but you need at least three to six months savings. I had three months and it was barely enough to stop the ship from sinking. Given the choice again I would have held off going freelance for one more month. That would have let me finish off the big client I had just landed and put me at six months income in the bank.

I too got caught up in the excitement of that big client and jumped just a bit early. It's great to celebrate your first big client, but don't let it get in the way of your objective to run your own amazing business.

As we'll discuss later — I don't think that there is ever enough cash in your bank account when you're freelancing. If you can hang on for just one more client and go with eight months or one year of income, then do it.

The bigger the crash pad the softer the landing into becoming a proper business. One more month of extra hours is worth the safety net you're building.

Partner Support

If you're not in a long term relationship or married, this next chunk isn't for you. You can skip ahead and just know that your partner better be 100% on board with your freelancing.

Your spouse/partner is your first business partner. They may not be involved in the day to day business activities, but they're still your business partner. If you think different, you're wrong.

That means right out of the gate you need to watch how you

speak about the business. It's not **my** business, it's **our** business. Your spouse/partner is involved from day one and their life hinges on the success of it as much as your life does.

The best support I've had during my freelance career is my amazing wife Cynthia. She believed that I could build a business and support our growing family. She was all in to make the freelance jump when I had the savings that we had agreed on and had a few clients lined up. She continually says how much happier I am, and she is, because I run my own business that can flex with our family schedule.

She loves that I can jump in at homeschool time which lets her go for a run. She loves that I can take our kids to the skating club and watch them skate while she coaches them and then play while she coaches the next session.

My wife is one of the best people I have to bounce ideas off of. She is a great resource when I'm not sure about taking on a client. She's been right about poor clients when I didn't see it, and I've paid for not listening to her.

Without your partner fully invested in the business, you're much more likely to fail. When you need just a few extra hours one night, they'll resent the time. When you're having a tough day, they'll tell you to get a job.

That attitude will bring you down. You need to make sure that you dig in together and get behind the business you want to run. You better know what type of life they want to lead and what type of business they want to see.

Assessing Risk

The biggest hurdle to your partner supporting your business is usually their comfort with risk. If one of their parents had their own business and all they can remember is barely making ends meet each month, they're likely going to be adverse to the risk. All they've seen so far is a hobby that wore the mask of a business.

If their parents ran a successful business and they were provided for, it's likely that they will jump right in behind you on the freelance band wagon. They've seen how freeing being your own boss can be and they'll be ready for the long days that need to happen from time to time.

I had one coaching client who was mad that their spouse wasn't on board with the new business. When I say on board I mean that she was yelling about the "terrible" business many times a week. My client was baffled by this because it seemed so out of proportion to what he was doing. So we talked to his wife.

Turns out, my client wasn't quite truthful with himself. Oh, he was right, his spouse hated the business. He just lied about not knowing why.

See he had started other businesses. He had spent through their savings once before. He had quit a job and then "went to work" every morning for months to work on his latest idea.

The only thing his wife would give him this time is that he hired a coach to help him instead of just flying by the seat of his pants. He still hadn't talked to her first about the expense of hiring a coach in the first place.

It was a very awkward conversation since I was the coach.

We did negotiate some time for his work. I also promised that I wouldn't let him pay for more coaching unless she called me to allow it.

That may sound harsh, and we didn't quite hit the revenue numbers she wanted to see. But we were close and she was happy at the end of six months. They had a better marriage because we planned weekly meetings to talk with her about the business.

At the end of 6 months there was no more coaching, but in an exit call with both of them they were so much happier. They were both willing to make sacrifices for the business, and they had a marriage built on solid communication.

ONE OF THE BIGGEST WINS OF MY COACHING CAREER!!!

Getting Your Partner On Board

If you have the risk adverse partner then you'll need to sit down together and address the risks they see. You'll have to have a serious talk about how the business will run. You'll both have to understand the expectations of each other if you want to move forward.

I'd strongly suggest that the two of you decide how much savings you need before you jump out on your own. If you want three months and your spouse wants six months, go with six months. If you think six will do and they feel more comfortable with a year, go with a year.

The rule of thumb is that you go with whatever number the more risk averse person wants, within reason of course. If they say they want five years of income saved when you feel that six months is good, then it's going to take many serious talks to sort out what risks they see that they don't like.

When your spouse/partner comes up with that huge time frame, they're likely dealing with another fear. It's unlikely that they care so much about 5-years, they're just scared and that's how they're dealing with it.

You need to take the time to dig in deep and figure out what the fear is. Once you understand the fear properly, you can address it together. Yes, it may take months to do this, but you're business is much more likely to win if your spouse/partner is on board.

Once you've agreed about how much savings is needed, you both need to set a plan to get there. Cynthia and I decided that I'd work every night except Friday and Saturday (she worked Saturday so I could work all day at home) and all day Sunday. She also offered to take on many of the chores around the house for six months so that I could get the business going. We, as a team, decided that me going freelance was what we wanted. We made a plan and then executed on it.

I've talked to other freelancer's that had two high incomes decide that 10% of the family budget would go into the savings account for the business to build it up. The business needed to be running well to make the jump, but they built up the cushion with their own income as well. This had the side benefit of getting them comfortable with living on 10% less.

If you can learn to live on less before you head out on your own, you'll be ready for the lean times. Don't fool yourself into thinking you won't have lean times. They will come in any business so you need to be ready.

Once you have an agreement for a savings level, write it down. Put it on the fridge and track your progress towards it. Yup, we had one of those thermometer drawings on the fridge.

Tracking the progress makes it tangible. You can see what the sacrifices you are making are leading towards. It helps make it easier as one of you does the dishes, or puts the kids to bed on your own. Each addition to the goal is earned by both of you.

Billing

Partner on board? Check!

Savings set? Check!

Doing work is one thing. Getting paid for it is something totally different. Make sure you have a good billing system set up before you jump out on your own. Having cash coming in the business, is what will keep it living.

There are lots of great options for invoicing software around. I currently use Cushion[1], but have used and liked 17Hats[2], Ronin[3], Cashboard, Harvest[4], Solo[5], Freckle[6], and when I started I used a single piece of desktop software called Billings[7]. The biggest advantage to Billings the single payment I could afford at the time instead of the monthly fee I'd have to keep affording.

While you're still working that regular job, take the time to evaluate which option works best for you. Talk to other freelancers that you know and ask what they use. Why do they use it? What do they love about it? What do they hate about their billing software. Choose one and stick with it for at least a year. It's only after a year of working with a tool that you can identify any issue with it.

I'm not giving you permission to move to the hottest new tool after a year though. Take a hard look at the problems you have with your billing software and then look for something that solves those problems without introducing a whole host of others that will bug you more.

There are things I don't like about Cushion, but all in all, I haven't found other software that solves those problems and doesn't add a whole bunch of other issues that would bug me more.

Project Management

Partner on board? Check!

Savings set? Check!

Billing system in place? Check!

Now what about project management?

When I started I used OmniFocus[8] as my task manager and project manager. I didn't really involve my clients in a project management system. We used email.

That started to fail me and for years I used Redbooth[9], until they changed their pricing which would have doubled what I paid, so I went back to Trello[10].

While I may have tried a number of things over the years, I stick to the same ideas around new software as I told you with billing software. Identify the problems you're having and then look at new options. **Only** change if a new option fixes the issues without introducing other problems.

One thing to remember with any software you use, if you're not paying for the service then it's not likely to stay around. It's also quite possible that you're the product. Make sure you know what the business model is of the software you use, and that you're the client[11]. I've seen many great options die on the vine because they didn't get some round of VC funding and they weren't actually profitable.

Don't get left scrambling to find a new option.

Some other options are:

- Asana[12]
- Basecamp[13]
- Teamwork[14]
- Clubhouse.io[15]
- ClickUp[16]

Just like with billing software, some people love and hate each one. Read some reviews and decide which one you get. Then stick with it. If you can get away with something like OmniFocus or a Bullet Journal[17], then do it. They don't require recurring payments and the name of the game when you're starting is minimizing expenses.

Something Has To Give

Partner on board? Check!

Savings set? Check!

Billing system in place? Check!

Project Management system picked? Check!

With all this stuff set, you still don't leave your job. You shouldn't be leaving your job until you just can't stretch life any further to make a job and a freelance business work.

That means you have so much work for the next few months (as in paid clients lined up) that you simply can't run the business and have a job at the same time. Once you're at that point, and you can probably do more than you think, give in your notice and pull a few more weeks of late nights.

Then you're done.

Leaving when you think you have enough savings but you don't have enough work lined up will mean that you burn through your savings. I was lucky that a friend had a web development shop that moved 100% into selling products. They referred clients to me instead of helping them. Without those referrals the three months savings I had wouldn't have been enough.

I didn't have enough marketing or a reputation yet so my name couldn't carry the business like it does now. You may not have that profile either so make sure you're building it now and that you have work lined up for at least a few months before you take the leap.

Most freelancer's won't admit that luck was a factor and that they barely planned their launch. Don't be like that. Plan the launch and stick with the job longer than you think you can.

Now You're Ready

Partner on board? Check!

Savings set? Check!

Billing system in place? Check!

Project management system set? Check!

Work booked out for a few months? Check!

WOOOOHOO, you're ready to jump out and freelance.

Enjoy the ride. It's a wild one.

Other Resources

Here are some other resources you should read before you jump out on your own.

- The $100 Startup[18]
- Entreleadership[19]
- Start[20] and Quitter[21] by Jon Acuff
- 48 Days to the Work You Love[22] (my most gifted book)
- Clockwork[23]

In this chapter I just walked you through all the things you need to have ready before you can think about going freelance. The next chapter is going to deal with one of the biggest mistakes I made in my first months of going on my own.

I wasn't serious about my time.

TWO
BEING REALISTIC ABOUT THE TIME YOU'LL WORK

* * *

When I started freelancing a 'huge' project was $5k. When I say huge, I mean that I dreamed of getting projects that big. I would throw myself a private dance party and call my wife to celebrate. The dance party would be private mainly because I look much like Elaine from Seinfeld when I dance. A full body dry heave set to music.

I knew that a $5k project was ultimately not that big in the realm of web projects. When I was working in house for a non-profit I had awarded projects for $20k. I wanted to be the type of business that could get projects for that much. My typical project was in the $2k range. If you're just starting, that may even seem large. My first project was $900 and I was a bit shocked someone would let me design and build them a full website and support it for a year for such a high price.

My math starting was that I could get a few $2k projects done in a month, say 3. Three $2k projects meant $6k a month. That would put me at $72k in revenue for the year. That was three times my wage working at my in house job.

My reality was far from those dreams.

The big problem I had when I started is that I didn't have any idea of how to be realistic with the time I'd spend working in a day. I didn't understand how projects work, and that they usually take longer than you figured.

This chapter is going to give you the tools you'll need so that you can be realistic with your time.

The Project WILL Take Longer

One of the first things I learned was that most projects take longer than I thought. After 10 years of building sites, and learning to add padding — many projects still take longer than I figure.

Maybe it's only a day of extra time, but maybe it's a week. Maybe it's a month. If you're extra 'lucky' you'll get a call about a project the client never signed off on a year ago that you had cut your losses on. Now you get to start it back up because your contract doesn't let you say no.

The most common issue you'll have with projects is that the client will get content for the project late. You'll be waiting for images or text for weeks past when you expected them. Weeks past when they promised them. You can't finish and you can't bill until you have that content in though.

Typically your web project is not the only thing on your client's plate. If you're working for a larger business you may find that the person you talk to about getting content has to track down ten other people to get the content. None of those ten people have content as their top work priority.

Maybe it's not the client though. Maybe you didn't anticipate some of the technical challenges that came up during the project.

Maybe something happened at home and you had to miss a few days of work.

As I revamp this book I'm recently off 10 of 11 days with sick kids. I helped clean up vomit 14 times in 11 days. I was up for a few hours a night 9 times in 11 days. Needless to say, a bunch of my work didn't happen.

During the third read through of this book we moved our toddler to a "big kid" bed. She's been up three times every night and often brings her 4-year-old sister with her. Oh and we're moving in two weeks. I'm sure next month there will be some other reason that life decides I don't need to sleep much.

The reason that a project is behind doesn't really matter. Most projects take longer than you anticipate and you need to learn to plan for that. We'll go into more depth in later chapters about reviewing and identifying issues with projects so you can avoid them moving forward.

One of the best things I've done to kill scope creep and waiting on clients is to change how I bill. We'll cover that again later, but I bill on fixed dates so that the client must pay me by X day regardless of delays in the project.

You Won't Bill 8 Hour Days

Another fallacy that got busted pretty quick was that I could bill 8 hour days to clients.

When you work in an office, you are there from 9 - 5 which is an 8 hour day with a 60 minute lunch. That means you're getting paid to go get a coffee or use the bathroom. That 10 minutes you talked to your coworker is billed to the company even if it was about last night's sporting event. In that 8 hour paid day, you might work four hours. Really effective people work six hours.

When you're freelancing, you can only charge client for time that you're putting into their project. If you need another cup of coffee you're not going to be billing that time to a client. You better not be billing them when you talk to the mail person about the sporting event. All that time on Twitter and Facebook, is not billable to your clients.

Those things are probably obvious, but what about marketing time? Did you think that you had a sales and marketing team at your job whose sole purpose was to sell clients so you could do the work. Who is going to do that for you now? Who is going to pay you to do that sales call or that follow up email?

No one is going to pay you for that work and yet it still has to be done.

By the time you pull all those extra little items that 90% of beginning freelancers don't think about you'll be lucky to get in four hours a day billable to clients. If you really bust your butt, you're going to get six hours and at the end of the day you're going to feel like you went 8 rounds with a champion boxer.

If you're basing your finances off billing 8 hour days, you better be prepared to work 14 hours a day to get it. You better be prepared to feel exhausted all the time and do subpar work because you're spent. Long days are certainly doable in the short term, but research shows that after a few weeks of long days, you start doing less work than if you were putting in a regular working day.

Discipline

My first six months of freelancing went something like this:

- 8am - get out of bed
- 9am - sit down at my computer and check Twitter
- 10am - finally start to open email
- 11am - walk the dog because it's nice out
- 12pm - hrm lunch time
- 1pm - back at work, hey what's happening on Twitter?

- 1:30pm - crap I need to write some code
- 2pm - CRAP I need to write some code
- 3pm - whew, some work got done, what was that only an hour?
- 4pm - is the day over yet? I want to do something fun. (Insert whine voice)
- 5pm - sweet I'm done. How many hours did I bill? 1.5???? WTF happened?

Yes, then I'd rinse and repeat. Is it any wonder that three months was just barely enough to get me through?

I was lucky because I did have that three month runway. I was lucky because my friend stopped taking clients and sent work my way. I know of four people that started freelancing at the same time as me but never got past the lack of discipline and went back to working for companies they didn't like, doing work that wasn't inspiring. They needed to keep the lights on.

That new found freedom when you start your own business is awesome. You are your own boss and you can decide how and when you're going to work. You can decide who you are going to work with. No one can stop you from taking your dog for a walk in the sunshine.

All of those perks are the awesome parts of the freelance life. You should enjoy them from time to time. The issue is enjoying them every day.

The reality is that if you take those perks every day of the week you are never going to be doing any paid work. Your landlord doesn't care about your awesome career and all it's freedom. They care that the rent is paid on time.

The first thing you need to do is to establish a routine. Get up at 7am. Get to the office by 8 or 9am. Don't turn on Twitter or Facebook. Don't check email right away, do the most important thing for the day first. Spend a few hours working on that, then move on to the other things.

I currently divide my day up in to four 3-hour blocks.

1. 6am - 9am
2. 9am - 12pm
3. 12pm - 3pm
4. 3pm - 6pm

I spend 6am - 9am every morning not checking email. Not checking any social media. I start it with an hour of personal development work and then I work on my most important task of the day for two uninterrupted hours.

My phone is set to Do Not Disturb mode. I gets no notifications from anything. I don't setup iMessage on my Mac or my iPad. I sit down and do the work I need to do.

Then I may use my 9am - 12pm block to run or hang out with my kids. I get back to work from 12pm - 3pm and most days of the week that's it. We have family stuff to do, like figure skating for my two oldest which my wife coaches. I think that you should be as serious about being a parent as you are about your work, so I'm at their activities as often as possible.

Find your routine and set it right away. Set yourself up for working deeply without distractions. I'm working without distractions right now on a Greyhound bus with terrible WiFi. You won't see a bunch of complaints from me because it let me revise this book, write a script for a video course I'm launching and compile the starting resources for two other books I want to write.

That was 4 hours of focused work. About 15000 words written and revised.

Don't wait months for your routine. Begin setting it up now so that when you make the jump, you land well.

You Need to Rest Properly

If you want to be productive, the whole thing starts with rest. Like I said, I start at 6am most days. That means I go to bed at 9pm...maybe 9:30 if I'm being wild. I do this because rest is so important to being effective during the day.

I've already said it, but burning the candle at both ends is only a sign that you're crappy at being effective in the regular work day. I work six hours a day and in the last 12 months I launched.

- 10 client sites
- 3 books
- 2 video courses
- 48 book reviews (that means I read the books too)
- Took a month off

I'm not doing all that on crazy hours and little sleep due to working late. I'm doing that by heading to bed early so I can get as much sleep as life and kids allow. This lets me be fresh and give my good creative brain the maximum possibility to focus and produce awesome work.

I cover this whole topic deeper in my other book The Art of Focus[1], but here is a summary of what good rest looks like.

- Get 7 - 9 hours of sleep a night because that's what you **need**
- Shut your screens off at least an hour before bed
- No work at least 2 hours before bed
- No caffeine 5 hours before bed
- No food 3 hours before bed
- Take a 20 minute power nap in the day

Then shut off all the distractions and when it's time to work, just do the work. Stop fooling yourself in to thinking that hours back and forth on social media is "work". Sure it may create some opportunities, but unless you're a social media manager, no one is paying you by the word to write there.

Other Resources

To help you get focused and do awesome work, here are some other resources.

- Deep Work[2]
- Pomodoro Technique[3]
- Getting Things Done[4]
- The Art of Focus[5]
- Rest[6]

Now that you can be realistic about the time things are going to take and you have a plan to maximize your productive hours, we can start talking about what you should be charging.

How to charge properly for your services is the focus of the next chapter.

THREE

CHARGING PROPERLY FOR YOUR SERVICES

* * *

Pricing is something that's not easy to get right at any point in your business. It's especially hard when you're starting out because you have almost no experience pricing things for clients.

As I mentioned already, my first real billable client was $900 for the site that I designed and developed and agreed to support for a year. Yup, you read that right. Nine Hundred big ones for all that work. I was excited about that first cheque for $900 though. I even felt like a bit of a fraud for asking for $900 to do the work.

In this chapter we're going to talk about the different pricing methods you can use. Why amateur's charge hourly, and I'm going to give you the recommendation you need to start earning more right away with your freelance business.

Amateur's Charge Hourly

It's inevitable that a client will ask what your hourly rate is. I'm telling you that amateur's charge hourly. Not only is it a bad idea for you to charge hourly, it puts your incentives in the wrong spot for your clients.

Hourly pricing means that no matter how fast you get at something, you really don't get a reward for it. Let's say that when you start building websites you take 20 hours to build a site and charge $100/hour. That puts the client bill at $2000 for the site.

Now roll forward six months. You've built up a code library and can build that same site in 15 hours. If we assume the same hourly rate you're now billing clients $1500 for the same amount of work. The fact is that 90% of the time, you're actually providing more value than you were 6-months ago, but your making less.

Seems like a bad deal for someone.

Charging hourly for your work also puts your motivations in a bad spot for your clients. What if your leaf blower just died and it's the fall. You've got leaves everywhere and who wants to rake? You saw a new leaf blower on sale for $150. What's to stop you from taking an extra 1.5 hours on a project and billing it to a client?

Oh I know you're trustworthy, but we're all going to be tempted when the situation turns out like that. Your client is going to wonder as well.

The point is, that when you're billing hourly, you're motivated to make things take longer to earn more. Your client is motivated to try and convince you that it won't take quite so long, so that they get a better price.

You have just made an adversary of your client.

If you're not going to charge hourly though, how will you bill for your work?

Flat Rate

Charging flat rate, or value based pricing is actually just a bit different. Flat rate is usually the first change that most freelancers make to their billing structure. Using the example above, you keep charging $2000 for a site and because you're getting faster you earn more for the work.

Going with flat rate pricing also means that clients have a fixed budget. They aren't just looking at their funds dwindle while you work away, happy as a pig in mud. They know that you're not inflating the time things take to earn a bit more. They can budget on flat rate pricing.

There are a few drawbacks to flat rate pricing is that it's on a fixed scope of work. That means that the client wants you to do A B C and you estimate on it. If they decide that really D is more important than C, you have to go back and revisit the statement of work. You have to revise it and produce a new contract with the amendments.

This compounds the fact that you and your client may disagree on what was in the original scope of work. It's not usually someone's fault. Your client thought that you would be able to fix their site at the drop of a hat for years, and you didn't expect that to be part of the work.

Often if you have a sane discussion about the disagreement it becomes clear to both parties where the error was and the issue can be resolved. But you both just wasted precious time. Often unpaid time on your part. I hate wasting time and I hate unbillable time creeping into my work day.

There really isn't a way around this issue. No matter how detailed you are with the spec, things change. After weeks on a project, you understand it better and can make better decisions than you could when you started.

A second draw back is that typical billing agreements in flat rate pricing leave you exposed. You take a 50% deposit at the beginning. You start winning like a boss flush with cash. The client is super exposed with all that money in your pocket. You could just walk away.

Further, if the client isn't happy with your services after you've done 10% of the work, they may just stick with you because you have the deposit. I don't know about you, but I don't want to be working with someone thats' not a great match just because I happen to have some of their money. They are likely to be difficult and I'm not very likely to continue to be interested in the work. That means the project is going to take much longer than anticipated.

At the end, when you're 90% done you're also 40% exposed. That last 10% is often the hardest part of trying to finish off a project. Everything needs one last tweak. Things keep taking time and you look at your bank account and realize that the mortgage is due and you need that final 50% payment. Needing that 50% can be a scary place to be.

After reading the drawbacks I'm not trying to discourage you from using flat rate pricing. I'm trying to highlight the issues so that we can talk about the next pricing method, and how I bill with it, because I love it so much more.

Value Based Pricing

At the end of the day flat rate pricing and value pricing are fairly similar. You come up with a single price that the client has to pay with both methods. The big difference between flat rate and value based pricing is that you might charge different amounts for the same work.

Often with flat rate pricing you would charge $2500 for a site build. The next client would get the same price point for similar work and scope. Where value based pricing differs is as you discuss with the prospect how much value they'll get from the work.

Let's say you build a new site for a barber shop. It's a local site and the value they get via new clients is a few thousand dollars a quarter. It's a decent boost but in the course of a year they may make $10k. Charing $2500 or $3000 is a decent price. They make 3x on the investment.

What if you do the same work for a digital product seller and with your new theme they make $10k a month? That's $120k a year. In that context charging $10k for the work still means they make a huge multiple on the investment.

With value based pricing you key your price to the value that you provide for your client. Not on the inputs you bring to the table. This is often used with companies that do conversion optimization. They will bill a flat rate of $X and then if they bring in an increase in conversions of, say 20%, they get an extra bonus. They're only paid that bonus **if** they bring in more than a 20% increase in conversion.

Usually if the client wanted to not pay the percentage, the initial fees would be much higher. Maybe the $5k flat rate becomes $20k. By keying your pricing off the increase, you're taking a risk and removing it from your client.

But How Do You Bill The Client?

Pricing and billing are different. Pricing is how you determine what to charge. Billing is the terms under which you get money from your clients.

As I said, often people go for 50% up front and 50% on completion. For a big enough project they may do 50% up front 30% at a three week milestone and 20% on completion.

All of these methods are serviceable, but there is a better way. One of the questions I get asked often is how do you move from one off projects to retainers with clients? How do you smooth out your cash flow. I know I have trouble spending when I have a big lump payment. Having many smaller payments spread out is a much easier way for me to manage my finances.

To that end, start your relationship by coming up with a price and a timeline and then tell your client that you're charging on retainer. Say the project is $10k and will take four months. You're charging a retainer of $2.5k/month with the guarantee that you'll get the original scope done in four months.

Because your client is already used to paying on a retainer, it's a much easier proposition to get them to move to a smaller retainer for maintenance and updates and further development time after the initial project is done.

I've done a few interviews with people and the biggest hurdle to making this move is always offering your prospects an option of the regular old flat rate pricing that they're used to. Don't hedge your bets. Start on a retainer and then you'll convert more clients to retainers later.

Below you'll find two great interviews about moving to recurring work with clients.

- Moving to Retainers with Mario Peshev[1]
- From One Off Client Projects to Recurring Clients with Jason Resnick[2]

One of the keys in both interviews is that Mario and Jason found it hard to get retainers when they presented any other option. Mario in particular, tried a few times to get people on retainer and it didn't happen. Then they went back to their old billing methods until they had the guts to only offer retainers for all work with them. Once they made that transition, people said yes to retainers without any other questions.

You Should Be Losing On Price

Yes that title sounds totally counter intuitive, but it's true. If every time you send out a proposal or discuss your fees, a client jumps in with a big 'yes', you're not charging enough.

When I started out my hourly rate was $50. Yes I too started charging hourly and I thought I was charging so so much. I had lots of bad clients that wanted everything in the scope plus three things they'd spring on me at the end that were never in the spec at all.

Of course they'd hold the payment over my head unless I did those three extra things.

When I raised my rates to $75 so many of those problems went away. Almost none of my clients asked for free stuff anymore.

When I raised my rates to $150, clients started expecting to be charged for research time and if the project took longer they expected that they may get charged more.

With each of these rate increases, I did loose some clients off the bottom of my stack. They weren't willing to pay my new rates. I still get queries for projects that are very low budget sometimes but when I state that my project minimum is $5000 those inquires stop in their tracks. The few that reach out anyway are often amazing clients and take an appropriately professional tone. This means I may take the project that was slightly under my usual floor.

Each time I've raised my rates I've got better work that required less project management time. Clients had more reasonable expectations of what I'd provide. They realized that I was a professional and should be treated as such.

I started treating myself like a professional, and my clients followed happily along.

I can't speak to everyone's field and their individual rates, so I'll stick to WordPress work since it's what I know best. If you're just starting out then maybe you only bring $50/hour of value. If you can work with bbPress, BuddyPress, AJAX Queries, the REST API, Gutenberg...then you should be looking at the $150/hour range.

When you're starting as a designer, maybe $1000 for a site design is valid. If you're providing a solid design process with wireframes and some user testing, branding documentation, content styles then you should be looking at a minimum of $5000 but $8000-$10,000 wouldn't be out of line.

If you're writing and you just bang off the required number of words then maybe $.10/word is what you're worth. If you're doing content research, customer research, looking at the tone of your clients, and then helping them make sure their content is effective you should be looking closer to $.25/word or higher.

If you've been providing good results for clients for more than a year, you're likely charging much too little for your work. Almost every freelancer I talk to is charging too little.

You may even be like me. I develop sites and end up doing a bunch of consulting about how you run your business and how you can be most effective with your work. I charge more for my work and my clients find value in it because they get this "extra" coaching. They leave with a site that not only is technically sound, they leave with a business on stronger footing all around.

Other Resources

Here are some other great resources that helped me understand the value I bring to the table.

- Pricing on Purpose[3]
- The Strategies and Tactics of Pricing[4]
- The Price is Right[5]

Now that you've got a handle on your pricing, it's time to look at the rest of your money management. I freely admit that if it wasn't for my wonderful wife, my business wouldn't be alive today. It would be under some pile of debt somewhere doing little to nothing.

With the information in the next chapter, I've seen business owners go from barely making ends meet, to feeling like they had freedom with their funds. They got out from under the weight of their business and could breath.

If you want to have sound financial footing, turn the page.

FOUR

HANDLING MONEY WELL FOR FREELANCER'S

* * *

This whole business thing comes down to money. You're trying to make it so you can keep a roof over you head and food in your belly. You want that fridge box to be a toy for your kids, not a viable shelter from rain. Hopefully at the end of all of it you've got some real profit. Not profit on paper your accountant says you have, but actual cash in the bank.

Most freelancers starting out just don't know how to handle money. Actually, 99% of the population of the world doesn't know how to handle their money properly. In this chapter we're going to cover how you should be handling your business finances.

Over the years I've used different systems to run my business budget. In some ways the system doesn't matter, the important part is that you have a system that is proven to work.

This chapter includes the system I've used to run my business to the healthiest profit it's had in 10 years. I get to work less and still bring in the same amount of income. It's nice to have that breathing room.

* * *

You Don't Need a Company Credit Card

Woohoo, you have a new company now let's make it really awesome be getting a credit card with the company name on it.

DON'T YOU'RE BEING AN IDIOT!!

If you have a credit card it's likely that you're spending 12 - 18% more than you would if you used cash. That holds true in Canada, the US, and any major developed country I've looked at (Australia, France, England I'm looking your way).

That's 12 - 18% that you could be saving for a rainy day and you're just throwing it away. Next you're going to talk about points and how your card gets awesome Air Miles, or something dumb like that.

You're fooling yourself if you think it's worth it. Credit card companies are a business. They're not offering rewards because it's good for you. They're offering rewards because it makes them more money. That means that the points you earn costs them less than the extra money you spend.

Let's do some simple math with the Air Miles we could collect on a Credit Card based on a typical Canadian flight for my family from BC to Ontario where my our lives.

A round trip flight for five of us costs around $4000. That same trip costs 2000 Air Miles per person. We earn 1 Air Mile for every $20 spent (and we would pay $75 a year for that privilege). That means to earn 2000 Air Miles per person I had to spend $200,000. Let's assume we're even lower than the average and only spend 12% extra on our cards. 12% of $200k is $24,000 dollars.

You just spent an extra $24,000 to earn Air Miles on your credit card. You could have bought the flight in cash and still had $20,000 in your bank account.

But what about purchase protection, online purchasing or paying for parking in major cities?

If you're in the US or Canadian you can use a Visa Debit card with few issues. Basically it lets you pay for everything out of your regular cash bank account but you get the protection of Visa. There are a few banks that allow this in Canada, and it's quite common in the US based on the US clients I talk to.

Years ago, when I switch from a regular credit card to a Visa Debit, I made a decent change to my spending. I cut out $60/month almost instantly once I realized that I had to transfer money on to it and spend cash, instead of credit. I had been wasting this $60 for months.

When you're freelancing, you can't be wasting any money. You need to tell your money where to go on purpose first if you want to stay solvent.

Have Extra Operating Capital

When you wanted to start a freelance business, you probably heard that you need 3 - 6 months of income saved before you make the jump. It probably took you 3 - 6 months to get things really going, even if you had a bunch of clients waiting when you left your job.

That 3 - 6 month rule holds true the whole time you run your business, not just when you're starting. In fact, I'd say that you need 6 months in the bank at the bare minimum. One year of operating expenses (including your salary) should be the goal.

That one year of funds is your emergency fund. How much would you stress about a client not paying an invoice if you could live for 1 year without earning another cent? How picky could you be about the clients you take on?

When I started my business, I burned through three months of savings. Then I didn't prioritize building up 3 - 6 months again. I had two very stressful years with just barely enough cash to pay myself. I'd get a bit of cash, and pay myself then spend wildly on whatever cool gear I wanted.

I remember driving to a local client on a Friday morning to get a cheque so I could pay myself Friday night. No, I didn't tell my wife that my 'coffee' date was really a way to get paid later.

Those years of stress were not worth it for the few extra things I purchased instead of saving.

When you're working to just barely be able to pay yourself, you can't make smart decisions. What if you get sick, can you really sit back and see what happens? You're already in survival mode, you don't have the luxury of being sick.

Now that I have 6 months of income (and working towards my full year) saved I don't have to stress about income. I put my head down and work the plan. I get to stay picky and wait for that truly good project with the client I want to work with, instead of working with whatever simply comes along.

What Is Your Emergency Fund For?

It's great to have the 6 months of income but what is that money really for? Let's start by saying what it's not for.

It's not for going to a conference. It's not for buying a new computer to replace the one you'd like to upgrade. Unless you suddenly break it and need to top up your savings for hardware replacement. It's not to purchase new software.

None of those things are emergencies. They're all things you should plan for and have savings for.

You should be budgeting to replace your tools every few years. Your computer will get old and will need replacement. That is not a surprise. Save your money for it.

Emergencies are when you accidentally drop your laptop, or it gets stolen. You have one year of operating expenses saved, so you go buy the one you need. Sure, it sucks to spend the money like that, but that is what an emergency fund is for.

Getting sick and needing to take a month off is an emergency. A relative dying and needing to book a flight is an emergency.

Anything that's not an emergency should be on your budget which we've already looked at.

Save 5% more

One of the biggest mistakes I see beginning freelancer's make (and one that I made) is not saving properly for their taxes.

In Canada my official tax rate is around 25%. By the time I count my write offs, it comes out closer to 15%. That means I save 15% at a minimum and more likely 20%.

When you run your own business you'll get to write off stuff like:

- Internet
- House expenses (based off how large your office space in the house is)
- Car expenses (based off mileage driven)
- Computer hardware and software

Even with those write offs, you'll owe the government money at the end of the year. It's not a surprise and you should be saving for it. If you're not saving for it, you're acting like a child. If at the end of the year you have extra saved that you didn't need to pay to the government, then you have extra money and you can celebrate.

Having extra money is not a bad thing.

I said at the beginning that you save 5% more. That extra 5% is just in case money. One year I had saved $5000 but then ended up with a $9000 bill. That meant on top of saving like I normally should,

I had to make payments out of me revenue. That was money I needed and the payments made the year really stressful.

Taking Profit First

Now the question is for most freelancers, what system should I be using to run my budget. For a long time I used Dave Ramsey's o based budgets. They were great to get me out of debt, but then they started to fail me in that I still didn't have much money left. I went looking for another system to take me the rest of the way and I found Profit First.

The basic idea of profit first is that you take your profit first in the business. To do that you divide all your money up by percentages. Here is what I've found works for digital professionals.

- Profit - 5%
- Owners Comp - 60%
- Operating Expenses - 20%
- Taxes - 15%

All the money starts in your 'cash' account every pay period. Then on the 10th and 25th you divide it up between these accounts. That's it.

If you don't have enough money in your operating expenses to purchase something, you don't do it. If you don't have enough money to pay yourself what you want to pay yourself, then you take a pay cut.

Yes this sounds painful. It's super painful to start but the constraints are going to help you build a business that is properly profitable. When you see the pain of not being able to pay yourself what you want, you know there is a sales problem and you start digging in to it so you can start paying yourself again.

When you see that you can't afford a new computer, you start looking at your sales, or your spending habits.

Constraints like this are the lifeblood of a well run business. Embrace the pain and use a system for your budget.

Other Resources

If you've read above and want to up your financial game at home and in the business, you should read these.

- Profit First[1]
- Financial Peace[2]
- The Total Money Makeover[3]
- The $100 Startup[4]
- You Need a Budget[5]

Now that you've got a system to keep your funds under control it's time to talk about how you deal with payments from other people. What type of boundaries do you set? What terms are usual? Can you negotiate with the companies on their payment terms?

All those questions and more will be answered in the next chapter.

FIVE

SETTING PROPER PAYMENT TERMS

* * *

You are not a bank, so don't let your clients treat you like one. What I mean is that you don't earn the bulk of your income via interest on money owed.

Unfortunately lots of people are going to try and treat you like a bank by paying late. Even worse, they are going to object to the late fees they agreed to at the beginning. This sucks, but you need to stick to your guns.

You should be dumping late payers in all but a very few scenarios.

I bill based on retainers now and as a grace, I give people 5 days to pay. That should give you enough time to put a cheque (yes us Canadians spell check funny) in the mail in Canada and for it to get to me. If you don't pay on time then I had 2% at 10 days and another 2% every 30 days until you've paid in full.

But when you're starting, you don't even know what's normal.

You don't know how bold you can be with your requests for payment and the terms under which you get paid.

Don't worry, I'm going to walk you through exactly how I have treated payment terms for years. How I never have late payments and get most of my work paid 100% up front.

Payment Exceptions

The great thing about running your own business is that you set the rules. If you want you can wave late fees. I had a client who's wife died. He didn't owe me much and had been a great client for a few years. We still get coffee together a few times a year because we enjoy talking. You can bet that I turned off all the late fees and we decided that I wouldn't bother him for a year on the project.

A year later we picked it back up and finished it out. I got my final payment then and I still get coffee with him.

Real life happens to you and to your clients. In light of that, flex your rules to make sure that you're a reasonable human. Long term clients that pay on time may get a late fee waived if they ask nicely on a single late payment, but that's it. If it becomes a problem they get late fees, and likely dropped.

Your Cashflow Is NOT My Problem

At some point you're likely to end up doing some subcontracting. I have found that agencies or other freelancers often ask to defer payments until they've been paid by the end client.

Never agree to that.

They're trying to treat you like a bank. They've borrowed against you and they want that loan interest free. All this shows is that they can't manage their business cashflow. They get the same payment terms as a regular client.

If the agency or freelancer signed your contract, they are the client and it's their responsibility to pay you on your terms. If they want to make payment dependent on the end client, then that end client should be signing your contract and paying you directly. That end client can work with your terms and the agency is cut out of the mix.

Sticking to my guns has meant that I've had to say no to some agencies that want me to work for them. It's unfortunate to lose some of those opportunities, but you and I don't run a bank. More often, the agency can make an exception if they really want you to work for them as an outside expert.

What About Coca-Cola?

What if some huge company like Coca-Cola calls you and wants you to work on their project? They're often going to have some contract that says 90 days till payment because some MBA that works for them has told them to keep their cash in their hands as long as possible.

For one large microchip design firm, I did take longer payment terms, but I pushed hard. They started at 60 days and I said no. Then they said 30 days, and I said no. Then they said they were allowed to 'rush' a payment and get it in 5 days. I said yes to that. The only reason I was able to get those payment terms was because I pushed, and I made sure I was talking to someone that could get those exceptions made, right from the beginning of my conversations with the company.

It's up to you if you take longer terms. Having cash in the business is important. A freelance business is not some huge company that can run a loss for years. When you start loosing money that can mean one project and your business is dead.

Pay Respectfully

Just like you expect to be paid respectfully, you should be paying respectfully. You should be paying any subcontractors you hire as soon as you agree the work is done.

Save 10% more than you agreed to pay a subcontractor at the beginning. It's not your money so move it to an account on it's own and the money sits there until the project is delivered.

Don't wait until your client pays you. The subcontractor signed a contract with you. You're the client. It's your responsibility to manage your cashflow and pay your contractors on time. Try to make sure that any contractors get paid within hours of sending an invoice.

You'll be disappointed to find out that most subcontractors you paid this way send an email astonished that you take care of them so fast. They expected to chase you. They thought that was normal. Working with you was the first time they got paid on time.

Who do you think they're going to want to work for next time? Who will they jump on a project for quickly? Who will they send work to if they can't handle it?

Live and Feed

I've told you to take a hard line on a bunch of stuff for payment and I firmly believe that you need to do this if you want a viable business. If you don't treat yourself like a business you're clients won't either.

With everything I say, I know that sometimes you need to feed your family. You need to keep a roof over your head. As long as it's not morally objectionable for you, then do what you need to do to live.

A few years before I started building websites I struggled to find and keep work. I applied for a job at a local coffee chain called Tim Horton's. I had more than one friend make some comment about working there being beneath them. They insisted that they'd never "sink so low" to work at Tim Horton's.

I suppose I should envy them for having so much pride?

I admit that it wasn't in my plan, but I will always do what keeps my family fed. I'll take a client that's not quite up to my normal guidelines. I'll take a slightly lower budget than I'd prefer.

I'll hang my pride on continually being able to feed my family.

Other Resources

- Fuck You, Pay Me[1]

Now it's really up to you to take this information and be bold with your requests. It's not really being bold though, it's treating yourself like a professional and expecting to get paid like a professional.

The next chapter is going to dive deeper into boundaries. How do you draw the distinction between clients and prospects? Is someone that once did work with you still a client or do they become prospects? What type of communication with your clients is reasonable? What about requests to "pick your brain?"

SIX

HOW TO SET BOUNDARIES WITH YOUR CLIENTS

* * *

Four days of the week I start work at 6 am and work until 9 am. Then I take a three hour break to run, or ride my bike. Maybe I'll take my older two kids to the library or help with homeschool. Maybe I'll take all my kids to the park and my wife will go for a run.

Then I get back at work from noon - 3 pm.

Friday my wife runs with a friend and I get up around 5:30am to journal a bit then handle getting two kids ready for school. My wife gets home just in time for me to **not** have to haul all three kids to school as I do drop offs. Then from 9am - 1pm Friday is devoted to any calls that need to happen. From 1pm - 3pm I head out to the coffee shop and do some business planning before I head to gymnastics with my oldest for 3:45pm.

Note that the only times I talk a call is on Friday, if there is room. If there isn't, then you have to wait. Sometimes that means you have to wait weeks to get on the phone with me.

In 2009, Paul Graham, wrote a great essay titled Maker's Schedule, Manager's Schedule[1]. In it he talks about Makers needing large swaths of time to do their amazing creative work. They need to have these big blocks of time to focus without interruption. That's why I don't take meetings and calls at other times in the week.

There's a great comic that shows the thinking that goes into programming and why you need a large chunk of time to focus. It's called "This Is Why You Shouldn't Interrupt A Programmer"[2]. In this comic the programmer goes from a small portion of the project in their head to a hugely complex set of items. Then someone comes to ask him about coffee and ... poof ... it's all gone. They have to spend the next 45 minutes getting their head back around the project in the same way.

Programmers are not the only ones that need large blocks of time to do awesome work. Designers need it. Writers need it. Developers need it. Anyone doing creative work needs it. Anyone that works in the knowledge economy[3] needs it so that they can do their deep thinking, which is the most valuable asset you produce[4].

If you're a freelancer, you also need to spend part of your time as a Manager. A manager has a discrete hour of time. An hour for a meeting. An hour to do emails. An hour for a phone call. An hour for lunch.

In general, interruptions don't break the flow of a manager. You just stop the email and pick it back up once the interruption is over.

You need to take calls with prospects so you can turn them into clients. You need to build proposals for those prospects so they become clients. You need to enter your receipts so your accountant can do your taxes. You have email to answer.

The big problem that many freelancers have, is that they operate in Manager mode by default. They sit back at the end of a day and wonder where it went. They didn't write the code that was needed. A writer's word count is abysmal, and pixels did not get pushed by designers.

They're really not sure what they even did.

You Need To Protect Your Time

Knowing that you need large blocks of time, you need to start your prospect interactions off on the right foot. That means when they get in touch with you about a project, you have a standard email to send them that asks them a bunch of questions like:

- Why are we doing this project now?
- Why is it more important than other things you could be doing?
- Who decides if this project moves forward?
- What is the budget you have allotted for the project?

My standard email has at least 9 questions. If you're interested in seeing it, I've provided it in my other book called Effective Client Email[5].

When a prospect reaches out to me, they must answer these questions to move forward with the project. We don't get on the phone unless they've answered the questions. Once we have the questions answered, I'll provide them with my schedule so we can talk further about the project.

I don't take random calls at 2 pm on a Thursday, because that's protected time for hard creative work. Every person that wants to get in touch with me gets a link to my schedule where they can book a call with me. Sometimes that means they wait two weeks to get on the phone with me.

Sometimes that means they wait three weeks because they tried to jump the process and get a call **right now** and I said no. While they tried to jump the process, my call times filled up.

You need to be intentional with your time and protect it so you can complete the hard creative work that clients are paying you for.

When a prospect gets annoyed, give them a short description of the Maker's Schedule and Manager's Schedule. Just like you're saying no to them so you can do hard creative work, you'll say no to the next prospect so that you can do the hard creative work for them while they're your client.

Treat Yourself Like A Business

Many freelancer's I coach tell me that they keep getting crazy requests from prospects for crazy amounts of money. Not good crazy amounts of money.

Just a few weeks ago a local freelancer asked what do to about a client pressuring them to put up a bunch of content today. They wanted this emergency support for about 50% of the regular price, because they had worked together at one point. The former client figured it was 'owed' to them because they had a prior working relationship.

The freelancer was already busy. Busier than they wanted to be in fact. They didn't have time to do the work. What they should have said was "Yes, but I can't get to the work until next week. And my rates are twice that." or maybe "Yes I can do that today, but it's 4x what you suggested as a rush rate."

I know that this freelancer regularly gets requests like this and they are going to keep coming until they decide to start running a business. If you don't treat yourself like a business, your prospects and clients won't treat you like a business either.

You don't negotiate the price of your coffee and jump the line because you want it now.

Your prospects shouldn't be doing that either. It only happens to you because you let them.

Fixed Costs

I think the rub here for many is that 99% of freelancers don't have tangible fixed costs on the work they do. It's not like going to purchase a TV from the store. A TV is a physical good and you recognize that the parts that when into it cost money. You realize that you must pay more than Best Buy did so that they can have a profit on the TV.

It's easier to recognize the value of a TV because you can touch it.

Much of the work that freelancers do is not something you can touch. You can't see the 10 years of experience that went into my work. You don't see the cost of my internet or the cost of my computer. You can't see the time I spent thinking about the problem and testing out a bunch of options to see what was the best way to tackle the problem.

All you see at the end of a project is that your site now does something it didn't before.

What we're really selling is our knowledge and experience. For a great programmer or designer or writer, the most valuable thing you have is your experience and your thinking on the problems your clients bring to you. The actual code you write, or words, or pixels you push, are the least valuable thing you provide.

Someone else could use the same software and colours, the same code editor or writing tool and not do a job anywhere near as good as you can. It's your knowledge and experience that makes you valuable.

Knowledge and experience that carry hundreds of hours of hard work and learning. Thousands of hours of learning. Thousands of mistakes and time spent solving the issues you got yourself into.

None of this is something you can touch.

When a prospect says I'm to expensive and wants a lower rate, what they're really saying is that I didn't show them that they're going to make at least 3x on the pricing I charge. They're telling me that they don't see the value in my work, and that's a sales problem.

* * *

You Don't Run a Free Hug Factory

You probably give away too much work when you're starting. Here are some things that I charge for, that many freelancer's don't.

Reviewing Technical Systems Integration

So you have a WordPress site and want to integrate it with System B. You want to know how much it's going to cost to do the work and I'm going to charge you to figure that out.

I'm going to charge you to read the documentation. You're going to get a bill for a bit of demo code testing to make sure that we can in fact do what you want with WordPress and System B. At the end you'll get a report on what we can or can't do and how it matches up with your needs.

I charge for this because it takes hours of my valuable time. You can't evaluate the total cost of ownership of the work I'll provide without knowing how much it's going to take to build out your idea. So we need to research it.

You're free to take my report and demo code and shop it around to find a lower price if you want. But you're getting a bill for that report. Almost no one that's done a demo project that went successfully, decides to shop the work around later and go with someone else.

Picking My Brain

I charge for phone calls to 'pick your brain' about an idea. I'm happy to have a serious conversation about a project you want to move forward on, but I'm not around as a random sounding board for an idea you think might maybe go forward and possibly some day have some value to someone. As I've already said in this chapter, the most valuable thing you provide is your brain applied to a project, backed up by the experience you have. Giving this away for free to someone is crazy.

With prospects that look solid, we may take a few calls to sort out exactly what we'll be doing. All those calls happen at no charge. It's simply a cost of doing business.

But I'm not around as the token nerd that you run things by to then go shop the idea to the lowest bidder.

As soon as I started getting really strict about protecting my time, almost all of those prospects stopped getting in touch. None of them were willing to put in the effort to schedule a time that worked for me. They wanted me to jump to their availability. When any bit of friction was added to the equation, they bailed.

This was not a bad thing.

Proposals

No I don't come visit you and do a presentation about your site and how I could help you. At least I don't do it for free. Most of those presentations you're not going to win anyway. Usually they're tied to an RFP (stay far away from them) and what the company is really looking for is 2 suckers to make up the three proposals they're supposed to get.

They're going to go with the preferred contractor who helped write the RFP anyway. If you didn't help write the RFP, then don't bother with the RFP process. Move on to another prospect that views you as an expert.

The thing is that you have to charge other clients for the hours wasted on that futile presentation. I don't think it's fair and I don't want to waste my time at all. If you want to have an in person meeting with me on a project, you can pay me to show up, or come to visit me.

I want to work with clients that are interested in me as the expert. Not clients that need to fill in a required three proposals.

Other Resources

Before you can really set your boundaries you need to know your goals as well. Here are some great resources on boundaries and goal setting.

- Boundaries[6]
- Deep Work[7]
- Start With WHY[8]
- The 12 Week Year[9]
- The ONE Thing[10]

The hardest part about setting boundaries is convincing yourself that you're a professional and deserve the boundaries. You have the information now, so start setting those boundaries and make sure that you have reasonable work expectations.

But how do you keep your business on track to earn more? How do you grow your business? The next chapter is going to show you my goal setting strategies that took me from a struggling middle 5-Figure business to a healthy solo 6-Figure business.

SEVEN

SETTING AND ACHIEVING BUSINESS GOALS

* * *

The power of written goals that are public to people you trust, can't be underestimated. I ran my business for the first few years on cruise control and I owned a job. I had a hobby, not a business.

I want you to own a business, not a job. You're going to get there by using the goal setting strategies contained in this book. By the end of this chapter you should have your business goals defined and understand what it will take to get there. It will be up to you to build strategies to continue to execute though. I can't force you to follow through, so get some accountability you can trust.[1]

I'm going to share the **only** question I ask when I'm faced with a tough day and crunched time. This single question quickly defines the only thing I should be working on.

What Happened When I Started Setting Goals?

This isn't going to be a bunch of cliché sayings you've heard before about business goals. You need to be setting them, but not like most people tell you.

Most people, including myself, set yearly goals. You've heard that fitness studios have huge sign ups in December and January and then they're back to their previous attendance rates by February 15th.

Most business owners do the same things with their year goals. They work super hard at the beginning of the year and then two or three months in, they get tired. A big project comes up. They get a bit behind, and they start to figure that some time in the future they'll start to recover and hit their goals again.

They're lying to themselves. The best predictor of your future success, is what you're doing right now. If you're not doing the actions it will take to get you moving towards your goals now, then you're likely not going to miraculously start doing it tomorrow either.

So How Do I Set Goals Then?

The best way I've found to set and achieve goals in my 10 years in business, is to set them in 12 week increments. There is a great book called The 12 Week Year[2] that walks you through the whole process. I found it after I had been setting quarterly goals based on actions and it helped refine my process.

A bad goal is nebulous but those nebulous goals are what most people set. Something like "get more clients" is what you'll see written down. What is the definition of more. What can you control in that process? Can you actually make people work with you?

What is the ONE thing you can do in that process? What can you affect?

My prospect outreach goal is to reach out to three viable prospects per week. I can affect that, because it's an action I can take.

The more people I reach out to and talk to about coaching or development, the more likely it is that one of them will be interested in working with me.

One of them will say yes.

It's also easy to track goals like this. Did I reach out to three people or not? If I didn't, why not? I'm sitting here in a coffee shop at 3:30am on a Saturday morning after a two day conference. I made lots of initial contacts, which I'll reach back out to, but I didn't hit my second goal in the week which is "Invite 3 people into an introduction call".

Some weeks I don't hit that, and I step back and evaluate what I can do to make a change and hit that goal next week.

The thing with 12 weeks is that it's long enough to get real work done, but short enough to make you stay on track. A missed week is noticed right away. You're off your goals. With yearly goals, it's much easier to fool yourself into thinking that you can "make it up".

Have Accountability

At times I've published my goals on my site. At times I haven't, but I've always had accountability since I started goal setting. I've had a mastermind group for years. We meet twice a month, but I report on the actions I should be taking every week in our Slack channel.

They'll push me hard when I don't hit the goals.

My wife is also on board with my 12 week goals. At the end of 2017 we sat down and in the final 12 weeks planned to launch a bunch of products.

We decided that I'd work extra and have a set of weekly goals around product creation. We both agreed that we'd make sacrifices for me to hit these goals so that we can build the products that we want to carry us forward on income in 2018.

We sit down on Sunday nights and look over where I'm at with the product creation against where I should be. We look at the week and plan out how we're going to maximize my time in product creation.

She checks in during the week to see how each time block went.

Yes if you were wondering, Cynthia is amazing. I have no idea where I'd be without her, but I wouldn't be as successful as I am now.

What If I Miss My Actions and Goals?

The first question I ask my coaching clients when they miss goals in a week is, what happened. I only work with highly motivated people, so if they missed some actions there is almost always a reason.

I missed a bunch of my content creation goals in my first week executing the plan. In that first 11 days, I had sick kids 10 days. We cleaned up vomit 13 times in 10 days, most of it at some emergency time in the middle of the night.

So, yes I had a decent reason and we reworked the plan to maximize what I could do. I used my time travelling to a conference and back on a bus, plus a 3:30 am writing session in a dirty Tim Horton's in the heart of Vancouver while I wait for the morning bus to get home, to jump forward and compile the book content off my site. I'm using it right now to rewrite the updated version of this book.

I'll get back to recording the videos next week now that I finished revising the video scripts on that same bus ride. In total with my revised plan, I've written 21,000 words over three days.

Terrible internet on the bus was super helpful in not being distracted.

Focusing Question

When we needed to revise the content creation plan we started asking ourselves one big question: What is the ONE thing I can do with the resources I have available.... such that everything else becomes easier or unnecessary?

When I had a sick kid that my wife was dealing with and I was watching our two other kids, I used that question to revise my plan on the fly. I needed to help my oldest with her math so she kept moving forward in homeschool, and watch my middle child while my wife took care of a sick baby.

In that context, I couldn't do deep focused work. I had block towers to help build and math to watch along with hourly dance party breaks to orchestrate. What I could do is cut up all the content I had from coaching bootcamp, so that I knew what video scripts I needed to write.

I could grab the link in the admin area of my site to only the Book Review content in 2016 so that later I could look at the books I read and reviewed.

I could find the link in my analytics package to segment out my top content so I knew what the content of a book would be.

No I didn't rewrite all the video scripts, but I moved things around so that I could do work that was better suited to interrupted time and move my work forward.

The only question you need to start asking yourself is:

What is the ONE Thing I can do with XXXX such that everything else will become easier or unnecessary? Then build your systems around making that happen every day. Finish out the single task that will make the biggest change in your business, then worry about the rest of your work.

Other Resources

If you want a deeper dive into goal setting and finding your priorities, you must read these books.

- The 12 Week Year[3]
- The ONE Thing[4]
- The Art of Focus[5]

Stop, what was that one question again? If you don't remember, go back and read it. Better yet, write it down. If you can keep that single question at the top of your mind as you look through the next chapter, you're going to be so much better off.

The next chapter is all about reviewing your tasks and goals. People regularly switch task managers and 99% of the time, they end up with the same problems. They have way to much to do and no time to check off all the tasks.

It always comes down to a good review process. In the next chapter I'm going to tell you the exact review process I use to keep on top of my tasks. I do it every week so that nothing is ever out of my sight for long. By using it I don't end up with zombie projects that I have to rescue at the last minute.

EIGHT
STAYING ON TOP OF YOUR BUSINESS BY REVIEWING

* * *

I've read Getting Things Done by David Allen[1] many times. While I loved it and tried to stick with GTD methods, it always felt like it failed me. I wrote blog posts about how OmniFocus wasn't cutting it[2] as a task manager. I wrote a whole book on why a paper planner was a great option even in today's digital world[3].

You know what, paper had some issues to. As have a number of other task managers I tried. It turns out the problem wasn't with the tools, it was with me. My biggest mistake was that I didn't say NO enough, even after I wrote about NO being the most productive word in your vocabulary.[4]

The thing that made pretty much any task manager work, was doing my daily and weekly reviews.

I had the same issue with my business when it started. I'd continually feel like I worked more and more and more hours, but it never resulted in any more money in my bank account.

Turns out, what I needed was to review my projects and clients regularly.

* * *

Review Your Projects

Starting at one of the finer grained levels, let's talk about project review. There is a number of things you need to look at when you finish off a project.

Profitability

You run a business, not a hobby, so you need to make sure that every project you do pays the bills and turns a profit.

I use Toggl[5] to track the time I spend on everything. I'm running a timer right now at 4 am as I work on rewriting this book. Out of that I take the price I charge for a project and figure out my effective hourly rate. So if I was working hourly, what would my rate have been. I never want to see it dip below $250/hour, but I'm happy for it to go as high as possible.

Looking at each project briefly to see how much you made per hour will reveal mistakes you made and projects that you should never have been doing in the first place. If like many business owners you haven't been tracking your time, start today so that in a few weeks you can review it.

Identify

Now we have an idea of what we want to be evaluating we need to make sure that we're doing something useful with the information that we gather. If a project took a long time because the client wasn't getting back to you with the information that you needed, then you need to make sure that you have the information up front next time. Make any information that could hold you up a requirement up front before you start the project.

It took me a while to start enforcing this, but when I did projects started to go smoother and clients ended up happier with the project. We didn't get stuck somewhere in the middle waiting for information, everything moved forward every day of work. The important part is to identify any items that made the project less profitable, and put measures in place to make sure that they don't have a detrimental effect on the next project.

It's possible that the first few projects are not very profitable because you weren't that focused. You're the problem that needs to be fixed. What are you going to do about your lack of focus? How are you going to engineer your work environment to make sure that you can focus quickly and stay focused?

If you're not sure, there is a whole chapter on this in my book The Art of Focus[6].

How Often

You should be reviewing finished projects as soon as they are done. It's part of closing the project down. Thinking back after 3 months to figure out what held up a project is a futile endeavour. You'll never remember it accurately and what you think you remember will always be the client's fault because you're clearly faultless.

I sit down when I close a project and summarize how it went. What went well, what didn't go well. What can I do to make a project like this go better next time. All of these notes go in to a big text document and every quarter I look for trends in projects to see where I can get increases in productivity.

Reviewing the Big Picture

While project reviews should be done right after finishing them, other items can be left for quarterly reviews. One of the big questions I ask myself is WHY?

Why am I running my business?

Why am I writing books and building video courses?

Why am I involved in any of the podcasts I contribute to?

Why do I guest post on other sites?

Are these other avenues of getting my content out there producing the results I need them to produce to continue doing them?

Do I even know how to measure that effectively?

I'm running my business so I can have freedom to take my kid to figure skating at 3 pm. I run my business so I can use part of my morning to help out with homeschool. I run it so I can choose my workplace and hours.

I write guest posts to bring in more traffic to my site. Recently I went through all the guest post sites I contribute to in an effort to evaluate which ones bring in the best traffic to my site. I found that, almost none of them brought in any traffic of note. The best traffic came from podcast interviews I did, and content syndicated to Medium and added to a publication that I do not run.

All other guest blogging returned essentially no traffic to my site. So I cut all of it, but one site. It doesn't return much traffic, but whenever I get published on Addicted2Success[7], I get emails with other opportunities. These other opportunities are what make it worth continuing to submit articles to the site.

Cutting all of this effort that wasn't producing results means I can focus on the things that are producing results.

I do my own podcast because it's higher up the 'trust chain' than writing is. It's closer to shaking my hand, because you can hear my voice or if you watch on Youtube, you can see my face. This is why other podcasts yield a good return, people get to hear my voice and mannerisms so it builds trust faster than blogging does.

Clarity

When you answer these WHY questions, or the focusing question I presented last chapter, so many things start to fall into place. Taking a contract with an agency that wanted my time from 8 - 5 would mean I can't take time out to do homeschool with my daughter. It would mean I miss figure skating.

Looking at where I get traffic from brought more clarity to where I put my efforts in writing.

Regular reviews, with people to ask you hard questions is the foundation of making sure you have this clarity in the work you do. When you have clarity in what is moving the needle in your business, it gets so much easier to cut out the everything that doesn't help.

Other Resources

Yup, some of these have been recommended a few times now.

- Start with WHY[8]
- The ONE Thing[9]
- Getting Things Done[10]
- The Art of Focus[11]

Now that you have these tools in hand, it really is all your fault if you're feeling overwhelmed. It's up to you to do the review properly. If you can do your reviews properly, then you're going to get so much more done with your days.

It's up to you to tweak your environment and systems when your reviews reveal issues with your work. If you're not getting to your reviews, it's up to you to build a review process you can stick with.

The next chapter takes a bit of a different look at some of the same ideas. Instead of just talking about how to review your work, the next chapter is going to show you the process I use regularly to dig through all my ideas and find the right ones for my business. I'll share with you how I figure out which projects will bring the most benefit to me with the least amount of effort.

NINE

DECIDING WHAT THE RIGHT THINGS ARE IN YOUR BUSINESS

* * *

Ideas, ideas ideas. You've got lots of ideas. What you don't have is time to do them all this year. Sure over the next 20 years you can get so much done, but we generally overestimate how much we can get done in a year while underestimating what we can get done in a decade.

When I first started freelancing I had dreams of blogging about productivity and cycling and reviewing productivity software. I also wanted to write about nerdy WordPress topics to build my profile in the community. I did a bunch of it on different domains, sort of maybe consistently.

I spread myself much to thin and I was unable to gain much traction in any of the realms I was interested in. I wasn't consistent.

Compare that to now. I don't talk about WordPress nerdery. I almost never write about code, and the few times that I do it's never on my main domain. I always talk about ways to run your business in a manner that thrives and that allows your family/relationships to thrive alongside your business.

I've shut down my cycling site. I shut down the WordPress tutorial site. All of my content is focused around helping you run a thriving business. Once I did that, my production went way up. In 2016 I published 180k words on different sites. In 2017 I cleared 200k words on my site alone, plus a few books and a video course. 2018 has over 300k words published across my sites and the courses I've done, but that doesn't include the three books I published which put me well over 380k words in 2018.

All of these products and efforts focus towards one thing, helping you run that thriving business without leaving a path of destruction in your wake.

Part of me would still love to build a CRM/PM tool based on WordPress. But it doesn't fit into my focus currently, so I don't let myself spend time on it. That doesn't mean I won't build it, it just means I don't devote any of my working time to it. I don't even tack away on it in the evenings.

When I look at the top 20 things I have on my list, and then pair it down to 5, the only ones I work on is the top 5. The other 15 are only distractions from the top 5 and get no attention until I have accomplished one of the top 5. Then I evaluate it all again and choose a new top 5 items.

What To Do With All The Ideas?

It's great to say no to things but I firmly believe that you should keep the ideas around. When I have an idea for a course or book or plugin, I schedule 10 - 20 minutes to think about it and write down my thoughts on what it should be. Then I file that note away in Bear, and leave it for later review.

Every 12 weeks I sort back through the ideas I've had and decide if they are still worthwhile. Many of them head back to the trash heap. Some of them stay around to possibly work on in the future. Very few of them make it into the next 12 week cycle for me to focus on.

I walk you through the exact process I use to vet and then measure ideas in The Art of Focus[1] if you're looking for a system you can run with.

If you don't take the time to write down your ideas, two things are going to happen to them. First, you're going to forget about them. The rest of the day will fill your brain and you'll remember you had some great idea, but it's a vague memory now.

Second, you will continue to waste brain cycles trying to remember it. This will be to the detriment of the real hard work you should be focusing on. If I hadn't written an outline of the course I wanted to do, I wouldn't have had the 8 Week Business Bootcamp[2] coaching program I've been running in the last half of 2017.

Even if I remember it, the course you can get today wouldn't be nearly as good as what I reviewed for a few quarters and revised. It would still be that little shell I first thought of.

Once you've moved through a 12 week cycle, you can look at what ideas you have around and decide which ones are the ONE thing you should be focusing on in the next 12 week cycle. Which ONE will transform your business if you bring it to market.

Let the other one's sit until their turn comes.

You Don't Say NO Enough

Yes we're talking about NO again. It's that important.

The word NO is a scary one for many people to embrace. They feel like they're letting people down. We don't like letting people down, but if you want to have time to do things that matter, you have to use the word lots.

When I wrote the first edition of this book I said no to being a technical editor of a book for a friend. That was real money I could have earned to make sure the code was right in the book. I turned down that real money in favour of theoretical money I could earn on this book. It did turn out well. I earned more than double what I would have been paid to be a technical editor, but it was still a risk.

A few months back I had just finished launching a client site. Two weeks later they found issues with the site based on their business model assumptions. They wanted me to tackle the changes because I new the system. We had already finished their initial work and I had clients in my pipeline with deposits paid and my time booked out in the future.

I had to say no. I had no time to help them. If I had said yes, I would have served them poorly and I would have served the other clients that I had agreed to work with poorly.

You need to be comfortable saying no to clients in these situations.

When you know you're letting a client down, it's harder to sit down at your computer and do good work. It's rare that you work harder, you often avoid the hard work you know you need to do, because it's demoralizing.

Decide how much work you can take on each week and stick to it. Don't let a prospect push you into taking on more work faster than you can accomplish it. If you have to take more work because you need money, start charging more.

If you can't start doing this, you're going to burn out and everyone around you will lose out as you take time to recover.

Other Resources

- Boundaries[3]
- Rework[4]
- Hurry Slowly[5]
- The Art of Focus[6]

Yes I know you have ideas, and that's what I just showed you how to sort through. Keep some ideas around, but make sure that you focus on the ones that are going to provide the biggest impact in your business.

In the next chapter I'm going to ask you what type of business you're in. Oh you may think you know the answer, but you probably don't. Not understanding what type of business you're in can mean that you're on the path towards failure.

That's because, we're all in the same business.

TEN

UNDERSTANDING WHAT BUSINESS YOU'RE IN

* * *

You may think that you're a designer, but your not.

You're not a developer either.

You're not a content strategist.

While this may be the skill you sell, it's not the business you run.

Once you start running your own business you have one primary job...SALES. You run a marketing business, and the thing you market is yourself.

In this chapter I'm going to walk you through what it takes to handle the sales and marketing in your business well. If you can follow the advice here, and manage your time well, you can cut off so much of that feast and famine cycle that freelancer's complain about.

Sales

The fact of life for a business owner is that we are all in sales[1]. If you're at a job, you're trying to sell your boss on the value you bring to the organization.

When you're freelancing you need to get new projects that pay you well. If you don't then your business won't be able to keep a roof over your head. You won't have anything to eat. I don't know about you, but I like food and shelter.

Unfortunately being a salesperson evokes thoughts of some sleazy person selling you a used car that's going to break down shortly. They wear an ugly suit and probably have slicked back hair.

Before I was doing anything with computers but playing Diablo, my wife and I were looking at buying a truck. I went out to one lot and looked at a small Ford and ended up talking to an older guy about purchasing it. After talking for a bit he invited me inside to sign some papers and get the truck.

Here is where it all goes south, because I said I'd have to talk to my wife first and he told me that a 'real' man doesn't have to go talk to his wife about a car purchase.

Yes I walked off the lot and we have never been back. Even 10 years later when they had a vehicle we wanted on the lot and we had the cash for it...I refused to go to that dealership.

That's not the type of sales you should be doing.

Selling on Expertise and Value Creation

One of my key selling factors is my expertise. I've been building stuff on WordPress for 10 years. I've managed to build myself a nice little niche building WordPress membership sites. People come to me because they've been told by a few other developers that I'm the one to talk to about a project.

I continue to sell a prospect on my expertise in the initial call we have as we talk through the details of what they need and I can cite many other projects I've done that are similar.

I continue to sell them on my expertise with clients via the video testimonials on my site[2].

I continue to sell people on the fact that I'm more than just a coder, I can help them with a number of aspects of their business so they're more focused doing the work that will bring in the most profit, via writing on my site[3].

I continue to sell my expertise by being on podcasts like The Matt Report[4] or Freelance Transformation[5] or The Freelancer's Show[6]. I continue to build my expertise as I write for Liquid Web[7] and Godaddy[8].

I've found that selling on my expertise as more than just a developer is the best long term way to keep clients coming in at the rates I want to charge.

Building Your Expertise

If you're just starting out, you don't have any recognized expertise. You can't sell on something you don't have yet which means you have to ask yourself, how do you gain the expertise and recognition needed to sell?

The basic rule of thumb is that the closer you can get to shaking someone's hand, the more trust you're building.

To gain expert status with someone you may need 50 blog posts read. 10 podcasts listened to. Two times to meet them at a meetup. One time as a speaker at an event where you get to shake their hand.

If you want to scale your expertise fast, pitch conferences in your technical niche. Pitch conferences that your ideal clients will be attending. Get over the fear of speaking because it can help launch your business to success you never dreamed of.

After that, start blogging. Aim for publishing new content once a week on your site. Once you can write content your ideal clients will read once a week on your site, look at branching out to writing a few times a month on a reputable industry blog. That blog will help you jump the queue in your quest to get expert status.

Don't just focus on the ones in your technical niche, look for sites that your ideal client will frequent. Clients will purchase from you, peers will mostly just read your writing. Some will send referrals, but probably not as many as you think.

Every quarter look at what's working for you and keep the highest performers, cut the lower performers.

Sales is More

When you win a new project your sales process isn't done. At least it's not done if you want to have a sustainable long term business. My best clients are always referrals from past good clients. That means I need to continue to provide value and follow up through out the project and long after we've launched successfully.

We all start projects strong, because we're excited about them. Showing how amazing your value is means that you need to finish it as strong as you started. In fact, it means finishing stronger than you started. Dragging your feet on that last 10% will make the client feel like you're poor at your work even if the rest of the project went amazing.

Finishing off that last 10% well is all about customer service, which is what we're going to talk about next.

Customer Service

As I just finished saying, how you finish a project is more important than how you start the project. Getting that last 10% finished strong will mean that your client is ecstatic with your service. Ecstatic clients will yield more referrals. Ecstatic clients will yield better testimonials.

There is a study on colonoscopies that found that if you left the very uncomfortable tool in the patient for 30 seconds an the end of the procedure without moving it, they rated the procedure as less uncomfortable. Yes, 30 extra seconds at the end determined the overall rating of the procedure.

Even if the project goes poorly, but you impress the client at the end, you're likely building a long term client.

Communication is Key

The key to customer service is communication. More than getting the work done, communication with your client will win the day.

Two weeks ago I had sick kids for 10 of 11 days. We cleaned up vomit 13 times in those 10 days. Needless to say, I did not have the productive week that I had planned.

Then I spent the last three days at WooConf 2017. The internet on the bus was terrible, so I didn't do any client work. Lots of focused writing time, but no client work.

As soon as my kids were clearly going to be sick during the work week, I emailed all my clients to let them know I'd be a bit off that week.

They also knew that I was speaking at WooConf and would not be on top of much code, if any, while I was away.

Are projects behind? Yes. Are clients upset? Not at all, because I actively communicated with them a number of times about my status and how it affected the project.

Clients know that life comes up. They know you'll make a mistake from time to time. If you're clients get annoyed when something comes up once in a while, you did a bad job of vetting clients.

All they expect is that you communicate clearly with them instead of leaving them in the dark about what's going on.

Delaying communication when you're behind never works out. You get more stressed out about the project and then it's harder to even work on it at all. You get further behind and the call gets even harder to make.

99% of the time the call isn't nearly as bad as you thought it would be. Your client is happy you were honest and is willing to extend grace to you about the work.

After years of experience I firmly believe that most of the times I delayed communication, we could have salvaged everything with some clear up front communication. Your clients should know when they are going to hear from you, and should even feel like they get over communicated with on a project.

At a minimum they should be getting a Friday update recapping the week and outlining the plan for next week. They should be getting a Monday update telling them about the plan for the week. They should also be getting a weekly call with you to go over any rough patches.

Other Resources

- Book Yourself Solid[9]
- Get Clients Now[10]
- The Customer Service Survival Kit[11]
- High-Tech, High-Touch Customer Service[12]

I'm going to ask you a question now. Do you know what business you're in? I hope you said sales and marketing because that is the truth of it. If you don't take the advice here and start taking your sales and marketing seriously, you're heading for a business that struggles all the time.

The next chapter is going to continue this discussion by talking about the marketing tools you'll need to run a great business. As the chapter title says, you need to spend more time marketing. If you can't do that, then maybe it's time to get a job.

ELEVEN

YOU NEED TO SPEND MORE TIME MARKETING

* * *

We've talked a bit about sales already, but that was in the context of explaining the type of business you run. This chapter is going to talk about the concrete ways I've found to market my business over the long term.

Now I do little outbound prospecting. I don't call leads to tell them that I exist. Leads come to me through the marketing work I've done.

I'm going to share the tools that have worked for me so that you can dive in and use them for your business. Just because something worked for me doesn't mean you have to use it. Take it as advice and make your own tweaks to it.

Because something worked for me, doesn't mean it will work for you either. I started my business at a specific time in a specific market. When I started writing about WordPress development, there were few people doing a good job at it. No one was doing screencasts and written versions with screenshots. Now, there are a bunch of people writing about how to code well with WordPress.

It's also important to remember that good marketing will feel like you when your prospects encounter it. If it doesn't feel natural after you've been doing a marketing activity for a while, move to something else that does feel natural to you. You should be playing in the field that suits your personality and business, not the field that some guru said you need to be playing in.

Trust Velocity

I've already mentioned trust velocity as well. This is the idea that prospects buy based on trusting you, and that the closer you can get to shaking hands, the more trust your building with prospects.

One of the easiest places to start with your marketing is with blogging. It's a fairly low barrier to entry and it starts to get you comfortable with sharing your message.

Even though getting out and speaking at events yields more trust faster, it's easier to start with blogging or podcasting. Once your comfortable, then speaking is a great step.

Cold Prospecting

This is where most businesses start. You have no clients and no name. You're not getting referrals. You need clients so you have to start emailing people that have never heard about you and see if they want to work with you.

This type of marketing is fairly low on the trust velocity scale. You're contacting someone who has no idea you exist. They may not even have any budget for the type of project you'd do.

When I started I made a bookmark list of 15 job sites that seemed to be the best options. Not Craigslist or Elance, but sites like Authentic

Jobs[1] or jobs.wordpress.com[2]. Every day I'd go through the postings and try to contact 10 people about doing work. If I didn't have 10 contacts made then I'd look for other places to get in touch with people.

I looked at local businesses with terrible websites and sent them an email. Often I'd note a few things I saw that could be improved and send a link to an article explaining more about why they needed to fix the issue.

I'm not going to lie to you, I hated to send those emails. Cold calls were worse though.

Many of the clients that came through these methods were low quality. They had low budgets and wanted everything under the sun for those few pennies they were willing to part with.

My first goal was to eat and keep the business running so I took the work I knew was less than optimal. Most people aren't going to tell you that. They'll share a laptop at the beach picture, and not tell you that they are working on vacation, not choosing a cool spot to work. They won't tell you that they get paid more for sharing fancy pictures than they do for the work they were supposedly doing.

A very few of these cold contacts did turn out to be decent clients. I don't have any of them as clients now, but a few stayed with me for years via repeat business and they brought in some decent referrals.

Meetups

When I started my town had almost nothing going on in the technical space. Now, 10 years later there is a bunch going on in my town of 80k people. We have monthly tech meet ups, weekly maker days, and a whole host of other creative things going on.

When I started my only choice was to drive 1 - 2 hours (depending on traffic) to go to an event in Vancouver BC.

There was one local event that talked about general online business and by attending there and then teaching some basic WordPress stuff I was able to pick up three local clients for $3k total. No that's not much, but I didn't have three kids then and my wife was working, so it amounted to what I needed in a month.

I find face to face larger group marketing/networking exhausting. Yes I know that going to a WordCamp or other event to meet potential clients is what I need to do, but this is one area I struggle with.

I find I need almost a week to recover from going to an event like WooConf 2017, which was the week before I put the final touches on the first draft of this book.

Despite how hard I find it, I still think that I (and you) need to be making the effort to get out and meet people. It's far to easy for a developer or designer, or someone that sits behind their computer to stay behind that screen and figure that Twitter or Facebook is all the marketing they need to do.

It's hugely important to build relationships. Once someone has a relationship with you they are going to be more comfortable giving you money for your services.

Blogging

I wrote in a previous chapter about how I use blogging to show I'm an expert in my field. I won't bore you with restating all the points here. I'll just remind you.

- Start a blog
- Write content at least weekly
- Keep going through the long haul
- Tell people about your site because if you're not selling it no one is
- Find some decent sites to guest post on and measure the return you get from them

If you're looking for great resources on how to blog I highly recommend following Fizzle[3] and Copyblogger[4]. I also wrote a whole book that dives deeper into marketing called Finding and Marketing to Your Niche[5].

Evaluating Ads

Over the years I've been freelancing I've taken out a few ads for my business. I tried WordPress specific places and I've tried sites where I think that my target prospects will frequent.

I want to see at least a 10x return on the ads I send out.

I'll use an example of the ad I took out on WPPros, which is long dead. At the time it cost \$20/month. That means the total cost over the year was \$240. Let's assume that because of my listing in WPPros I made \$2400 which is 10x my investment.

The first think we have to do is take out the cost of the ad then our savings and taxes.

$2400 - 240 = $2160

$2160 - 15\% = $1836

Out of the \$2400 I truly got an extra \$1836 in sales. I still would have to figure that it took sales time on my end to come out of the end fees. This \$1836 is much less than the \$2400 you started with but most people don't figure on the costs that went into earning the extra \$2400.

I consider the math above simple a break even point for the ad. I'd likely continue doing it, but would be on the lookout for something that returned much better than 10x my ad spend.

It's highly likely that spending an hour or two guest posting for other sites would return at least the same amount, and these guest posts stick around bringing me authority and traffic for years where the ad is done when I stop paying for it.

Plugging Others in The Field

It may seem a bit counterintuitive to say, but a great long term way of getting business is to give business away to others. In theory these other developers or designers may be competition, right?

The truth is, that there is lots of work out there for good people. There are projects I like to do and projects I don't like to do. I may be capable of building a payment gateway, but I never want to do that so I send it to my friend Daniel.

I've always received more in return work when I plug other developers. In a few weeks or months they will have a project they can't handle or they don't like and I'll be one of the top people on their list to send work to.

Long term you build a bunch of fans that love sending you work. Fans sell for you way better than clients. Fans show up at 4 am to purchase tickets that go on sale at 6 pm.

If you're married the best way to keep a healthy relationship is to water the grass on your side of the fence. The only reason it looks greener elsewhere is that you're not watering your own grass.

People become fans because you're watering their grass. You stand near enough to them and while you water your grass you make sure that some of the water gets on their grass. When they start watering your grass a bit as well, you know you have a fan.

Unfortunately, this is not the fastest way to get your marketing going. You have to put time into consistently plugging others and helping them out before you start to see big rewards.

When I wrote the first version of this book I had spent 2 years consistently plugging others. It's been another 4 years now and I still see huge rewards. The people I helped out with work at the beginning now own huge plugins and send clients directly to me out of their support channels.

The hard early work has more than paid off hundreds of times.

You're Not Done Just Because You're Busy

I'm glad you've got some work and that your busy. DON'T STOP MARKETING. Many freelancers talk about feast/famine cycles. While some months are better than others, consistent marketing effort no matter how busy I am helps to make sure that the dips aren't as low as they could be.

You should be setting aside an hour or two every week, no matter how busy you are, to do your marketing work. At a minimum, keep your weekly blog post going and reach out to any leads that have come in.

I have one coaching client[6] who worked with me for two months. We mapped out his days and put in marketing time every week. We turned the business around from famine to feast. As soon as he stopped working with me he stopped putting his marketing time aside.

Over the next 4 months, he did almost no marketing because he was "too busy".

We're talking about working together again because he's back in the famine. It's an even bigger famine now though because he let it go so long, so he's trying to figure out how to even pay his people let alone me to help him.

If for some reason you really have to give up your marketing time in a week, you must replace it. If you don't, get ready for the famine and pain of not having enough work.

Other Resources

- Book Yourself Solid[7]
- Get Clients Now[8]
- The Brain Audit[9]
- Finding and Marketing To Your Niche[10]

Now you've got some tools to head out and do your marketing. If that sounds like a terrible idea. If the thought of marketing your business feels like jumping in a outhouse to you, then maybe you need to find someone to do that part for you.

If you're not telling people about your business, then no one is.

EPILOGUE

Like I said at the beginning, I want you to build a freelance business that kicks ass. I want you to launch into running your own business and win. I want you to get that freedom you desired.

The Freelancer's Guide to Getting Started gave you the areas you need to plan to make this happen.

Yes, you can launch a business without addressing finances. Yes, you could go freelance without your spouse on your side. Sure, you could start a business without having a project management system ready.

But you can't launch a **successful** business that sticks around for years without those things.

If you didn't take the time to plan based on the chapters you've read, then stop now and put some time on your calendar to do just that. If you don't set aside time to plan how your business will operate, then you're increasing your chances of failure.

If you're struggling to get your business launched, shoot me an email with your questions. I read and answer every single one.

My email: curtis@curtismchale.ca

Keep being awesome!

DON'T MISS THIS!

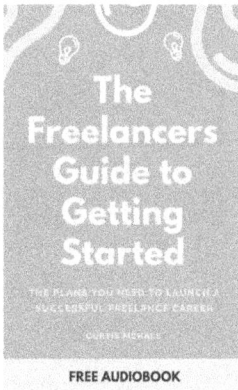

Don't forget that you can get the audiobook **FREE** by signing up for the email list at:

FREE AUDIOBOOK

https://curtismchale.ca/recommends/fggs-audio

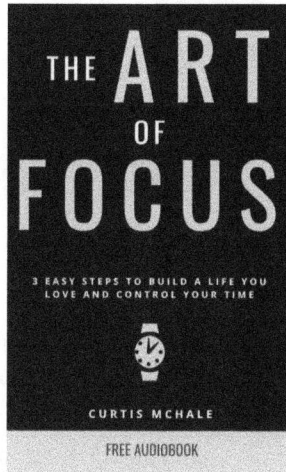

Analogue Productivity: Bring more value to work with paper and a pen

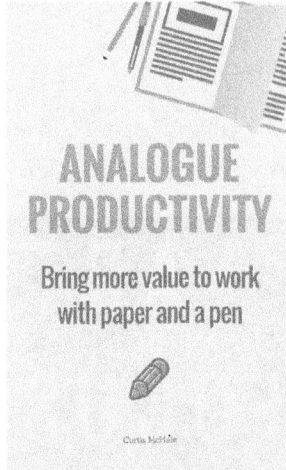

If you're always drowning under your digital task management tools, Analogue Productivity walks you through how I took the Bullet Journal System and built a system that keeps up with a digital business. You'll learn how I use it to make sure I cut all distraction from my day and get **good work** done, day in day out.

Purchase Analogue Productivity on Amazon

* * *

Getting Unstuck: The pieces you need to make your freelance business successful

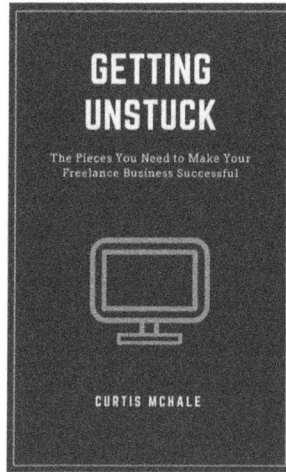

GETTING
UNSTUCK

The Pieces You Need to Make Your
Freelance Business Successful

CURTIS MCHALE

It's easy to feel stuck when your running your own business. Getting Unstuck gives you a step by step guide to stop running the freelance treadmill.

Get a plan to market your freelance business. A plan to manage your client relationships. A project management framework you can use today.

Purchase Getting Unstuck on Amazon

* * *

Becoming a Master: How to Stop Avoiding Hard Work and Become the Master You Long to Be

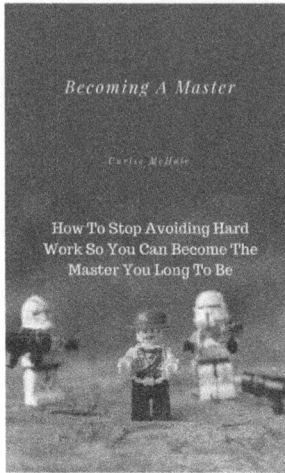

Becoming A Master

Curtis McHale

How To Stop Avoiding Hard
Work So You Can Become The
Master You Long To Be

We all want to master our fields, but it's so easy to get sidetracked on the way towards mastery. Curtis breaks down how to stay on track towards mastery and provides insights from multiple authors which will help you build a healthy habit of focus for work. No more working 80 hour weeks with little to show for it.

Purchase Becoming a Master on Amazon

ABOUT THE AUTHOR

Curtis McHale has one goal, to help business owners run a great business, and get to see their family. He believes that it's time to start putting as much focus on your life at home as you do on your work life. Doing anything else is simply waiting for trouble at home, which of course will affect how you do at work.

For more books and updates:
curtismchale.ca

Find Curtis everywhere: curtismchale.ca/find-me

NOTES

1. What You Need To Be Ready To Freelance

1. Cushion: https://cushionapp.com/
2. 17Hats: https://curtismchale.ca/recommends/17hats/
3. Ronin: https://www.roninapp.com/
4. Harvest: https://www.getharvest.com/
5. Thrive Solo: http://thrivesolo.com/
6. Freckle: https://letsfreckle.com/
7. Check out Billings Pro: https://www.marketcircle.com/billingspro/
8. OmniFocus: https://www.omnigroup.com/omnifocus/
9. Redbooth: https://curtismchale.ca/recommends/redbooth/
10. Trello: https://curtismchale.ca/recommends/trello/
11. Stick to software with a business model: http://curtismchale.ca/2012/04/16/stay-away-from-services-with-no-business-model/
12. Asana: https://curtismchale.ca/recommends/asana/
13. Basecamp: https://curtismchale.ca/recommends/basecamp/
14. Teamwork: https://www.teamwork.com/
15. Clubhous: https://clubhouse.io/
16. ClickUp: https://clickup.com/
17. I wrote a book an Analogue Productivity: https://curtismchale.ca/recommends/analogue-productivity
18. The $100 Startup: https://curtismchale.ca/recommends/the-100-startup/
19. EntreLeadership: https://curtismchale.ca/recommends/entreleadership/
20. Start: https://curtismchale.ca/recommends/start-2/
21. Quitter: https://curtismchale.ca/recommends/quitter/
22. 48 Days to the Work you Love: https://curtismchale.ca/recommends/48-days-work-love/
23. Clockwork: https://curtismchale.ca/recommends/clockwork/

2. Being Realistic About The Time You'll Work

1. Purchase The Art of Focus: https://curtismchale.ca/recommends/aof
2. Purchase Deep Work: https://curtismchale.ca/recommends/deep-work/
3. Purchase The Pomodoro Technique: https://curtismchale.ca/recommends/pomodoro-technique/
4. Purchase Getting Things Done: https://curtismchale.ca/recommends/getting-things-done-david-allen/

5. Purchase The Art of Focus: https://curtismchale.ca/recommends/aof
6. Purchase Rest: https://curtismchale.ca/recommends/rest/

3. Charging Properly For Your Services

1. Mario Peshev on retainers: https://curtismchale.ca/2017/02/03/moving-retainers-mario-peshev/
2. Recurring Clients with Jason Resnick: https://curtismchale.ca/2016/10/21/one-off-client-projects-recurring-clients-jason-resnick/
3. Purchase Pricing on Purpose: https://curtismchale.ca/recommends/pricing-purpose/
4. Purchase The Strategies and Tactics of Pricing: https://curtismchale.ca/recommends/strategy-tactics-pricing/
5. Purchase The Price is Right: http://chrislema.com/product/price-is-right/

4. Handling Money Well For Freelancer's

1. Purchase Profit First: https://curtismchale.ca/recommends/profit-first/
2. Purchase Financial Peace: https://curtismchale.ca/recommends/financial-peace/
3. Purchase The Total Money Makeover: https://curtismchale.ca/recommends/total-money-makeover/
4. Purchase The $100 Startup: https://curtismchale.ca/recommends/the-100-startup/
5. You Need a Budget: https://www.youneedabudget.com/

5. Setting Proper Payment Terms

1. Watch Fuck You, Pay Me: https://www.youtube.com/watch?v=jVkLVRt6c1U

6. How To Set Boundaries With Your Clients

1. Maker's Schedule, Manager's Schedule: http://www.paulgraham.com/makersschedule.html
2. This Is Why You Shouldn't Interrupt A Programmer: http://heeris.id.au/2013/this-is-why-you-shouldnt-interrupt-a-programmer/
3. Knowledge economy. (2018, September 24). Retrieved from https://en.wikipedia.org/wiki/Knowledge_economy
4. Curtis McHale. (2018, May 30). What is the most in demand freelance skill that will remain in demand? Retrieved from https://curtismchale.ca/2017/12/18/demand-freelance-skill-will-remain-demand/

5. Purchase Effective Client Email: https://curtismchale.ca/effective-client-email/
6. Purchase Boundaries: https://curtismchale.ca/recommends/boundaries/
7. Purchase Deep Work: https://curtismchale.ca/recommends/deep-work/
8. Purchase Start with WHY: https://curtismchale.ca/recommends/start/
9. Purchase The 12 Week Year: https://curtismchale.ca/recommends/12-week-year/
10. Purchase The ONE Thing: https://curtismchale.ca/recommends/the-one-thing/

7. Setting And Achieving Business Goals

1. If you're looking for some help you can send me an email and we can talk about how I can help you with your goals: curtis@curtismchale.ca
2. Purchase The 12 Week Year: https://curtismchale.ca/recommends/12-week-year/
3. Purchase The 12 Week Year: https://curtismchale.ca/recommends/12-week-year/
4. Purchase The ONE Thing: https://curtismchale.ca/recommends/the-one-thing/
5. Purchase The Art of Focus: https://curtismchale.ca/recommends/aof

8. Staying On Top Of Your Business By Reviewing

1. Purchase Getting Things Done on Amazon: https://curtismchale.ca/recommends/getting-things-done-david-allen/
2. Read why OmniFocus wasn't cutting it: http://curtismchale.ca/2012/12/06/omnifocus-isnt-quite-cutting-it/
3. Purchase Analogue Productivity: https://curtismchale.ca/recommends/analogue-productivity/
4. No is the most productive word: https://curtismchale.ca/2014/04/22/one-productivity-secret-thats-small-already/
5. Toggl time tracking https://curtismchale.ca/recommends/toggl/
6. Purchase The Art of Focus: https://curtismchale.ca/recommends/aof
7. Read Addicted 2 Success: http://addicted2success.com
8. Purchase Start with WHY: https://curtismchale.ca/recommends/start/
9. Purchase The ONE Thing: https://curtismchale.ca/recommends/the-one-thing/
10. Purchase Getting Things Done: https://curtismchale.ca/recommends/getting-things-done-david-allen/
11. Purchase The Art of Focus: https://curtismchale.ca/recommends/aof

9. Deciding What The Right Things Are In Your Business

1. Purchase The Art of Focus: https://curtismchale.ca/recommends/aof
2. Join bootcamp: https://curtismchale.ca/8-week-business-bootcamp/

3. Purchase Boundaries: https://curtismchale.ca/recommends/boundaries/
4. Purchase Rework: https://curtismchale.ca/recommends/rework/
5. The Hurry Slowly podcast will help you set sane work boundaries: http://hurryslowly.co
6. Purchase The Art of Focus: https://curtismchale.ca/recommends/aof

10. Understanding What Business You're In

1. You are a salesperson: https://krogsgard.com/2013/you-are-a-salesperson/
2. SFNdesign, WordPress Membership Sites: http://sfndesign.ca
3. I write about running a balanced business: https://curtismchale.ca
4. The Matt Report: https://mattreport.com/video-interview-wordpress-dev-curtis-mchale/
5. Freelance Transformation: https://freelancetransformation.com/blog/the-surprisingly-short-proposal-format-with-curtis-mchale
6. The Freelancer's Show: https://devchat.tv/show_host/curtis-mchale
7. My writing on Liquid Web: https://www.liquidweb.com/blog/author/cmchale/
8. My writing on Godaddy: https://ca.godaddy.com/blog/author/cmchale/
9. Purchase Book Yourself Solid: https://curtismchale.ca/recommends/book-solid/
10. Purchase Get Clients Now: https://curtismchale.ca/recommends/get-clients-now/
11. Purchase The Customer Service Survival Kit: https://curtismchale.ca/recommends/customer-service-survival-kit/
12. Purchase High-Tech, High-Touch Customer Service: https://curtismchale.ca/recommends/high-tech-high-touch-customer-service/

11. You Need To Spend More Time Marketing

1. Authentic Jobs: https://authenticjobs.com/
2. WordPress Jobs: https://jobs.wordpress.com
3. Fizzle: https://fizzle.co/sparkline
4. Copyblogger: https://www.copyblogger.com/
5. Purchase Finding and Marketing To Your Niche: https://curtismchale.ca/finding-marketing-niche/
6. Work with Me: https://curtismchale.ca/work-with-me
7. Purchase Book Yourself Solid: https://curtismchale.ca/recommends/book-solid/
8. Purchase Get Clients Now: https://curtismchale.ca/recommends/get-clients-now/
9. Purchase The Brain Audit: https://curtismchale.ca/recommends/the-brain-audit/
10. Purchase Finding and Marketing To Your Niche: https://curtismchale.ca/finding-marketing-niche/